Sports Illustrated KID$

STARS OF SPORTS

SABRINA

IONESCU

RISING BASKETBALL STAR

||| by Matt Chandler

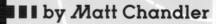

CAPSTONE PRESS
a capstone imprint

Published by Capstone Press, an imprint of Capstone
1710 Roe Crest Drive, North Mankato, Minnesota 56003
capstonepub.com

Library of Congress Cataloging-in-Publication Data
Names: Chandler, Matt, author. Title: Sabrina Ionescu : rising basketball star / by Matt Chandler.
Description: North Mankato, Minnesota : Capstone Press, 2022. | Series: Sports illustrated kids stars of sports |
Includes bibliographical references and index. | Audience: Ages 8-11 | Audience: Grades 4-6 |
Summary: "Around three years old, Sabrina Ionescu picked up a basketball. While she had natural talent, Ionescu worked hard. In middle school there weren't enough players for a girls' basketball team. Ionescu wasn't allowed on the boys' team, but she didn't give up. Instead, she recruited enough girls to make a team. Learn about how Ionescu became the first overall pick in the 2020 WNBA draft and the player she is today"— Provided by publisher.
Identifiers: LCCN 2021033324 (print) | LCCN 2021033325 (ebook) | ISBN 9781663983626 (hardcover) | ISBN 9781666323368 (paperback) | ISBN 9781666323375 (pdf) | ISBN 9781666323399 (kindle edition)
Subjects: LCSH: Ionescu, Sabrina, 1997-—Juvenile literature. | Women basketball players—United States—Biography—Juvenile literature. Classification: LCC GV884.I66 C53 2022 (print) | LCC GV884.I66 (ebook) | DDC 796.323092 [B]—dc23
LC record available at https://lccn.loc.gov/2021033324
LC ebook record available at https://lccn.loc.gov/2021033325

Editorial Credits
Editor: Christianne Jones; Designer: Bobbie Nuytten; Media Researcher: Morgan Walters;
Production Specialist: Laura Manthe

Source Notes
Page 8, "And now I use...," Sabrina Ionescu, "The Legend of Sabrina Ionescu," ESPN, March 16, 2020, https://www.espn.com/espn/feature/story/_/id/28878754/the-legend-sabrina-ionescu, Accessed June 24, 2021.
Page 10, "My middle school...," Sabrina Ionescu, "Her middle school said to play with dolls. She set an NCAA triple-double record instead." The Washington Post, February 4, 2019, https://www.washingtonpost.com/sports/2019/02/04/her-middle-school-said-play-with-dolls-she-set-an-ncaa-triple-double-record-instead/, Accessed June 24, 2021.
Page 12, "I wish I could...," Sabrina Ionescu, "Her middle school said to play with dolls. She set an NCAA triple-double record instead." The Washington Post, February 4, 2019, https://www.washingtonpost.com/sports/2019/02/04/her-middle-school-said-play-with-dolls-she-set-an-ncaa-triple-double-record-instead/, Accessed June 24, 2021.
Page 14, "Sabrina had her...," Kelly Sopak, "The Legend of Sabrina Ionescu," ESPN, March 16, 2020, https://www.espn.com/espn/feature/story/_/id/28878754/the-legend-sabrina-ionescu, Accessed June 24, 2021.
Page 14, "Yeah, she doesn't miss...," Eddy Ionescu, "The Legend of Sabrina Ionescu," ESPN, March 16, 2020, https://www.espn.com/espn/feature/story/_/id/28878754/the-legend-sabrina-ionescu, Accessed June 24, 2021.

TABLE OF CONTENTS

Words in **BOLD** are in the glossary.

RECORD SETTER

On February 24, 2020, the Oregon Ducks were leading the Stanford Cardinals by 18 points late in the third quarter. Basketball fans around the country were watching to see if Oregon senior Sabrina Ionescu could set a new record. In NCAA Division I basketball history, no player had ever scored 2,000 points and had 1,000 assists and 1,000 rebounds. Ionescu was one rebound away from making history.

⟩⟩⟩ Ionescu drives to the basket with the ball on February 24, 2020.

With the Cardinal on offense, Ionescu positioned herself under the basket. Cardinal guard Hannah Jump took a pass and launched a three-point shot. Her shot missed and went straight into Ionescu's hands. She had done it! The Ducks went on to win the game, 74–66. Oregon finished the 2019–20 season with a record of 31–2 thanks to the play of their record-setting senior.

>>> Ionescu celebrates with her teammates after breaking the NCAA basketball record and winning the game against Stanford.

CHAPTER ONE

CALIFORNIA TWIN

Sabrina Ionescu was born in Walnut Creek, California, on December 6, 1997. Her parents are immigrants from Romania. She also has a twin brother, Eddy, who shares her love for basketball. Sabrina and Eddy have an older brother, Andrei.

Sabrina and Eddy developed their love for the sport growing up. They often went to a park near their home and spent day after day playing basketball. They practiced nonstop. They played pickup games. They challenged players to games of H-O-R-S-E. They sometimes played against adults. The many hours spent on the courts helped Ionescu build her skills.

〉〉〉 Walnut Creek, California, is in the San Francisco Bay area. It is surrounded by hills and forested areas.

FACT

Ionescu speaks English and Romanian. She and her brother used to talk to each other in Romanian on the basketball court. It kept their opponents from knowing what the twins were going to do.

BROTHERLY LOVE

Though she has two brothers, Ionescu is extra close with her twin. They are self-described best friends. He has been her biggest fan throughout her life.

Ionescu says both of her brothers played hard against her. Eddy never took it easy on his sister on the basketball court. Eddy said many of their games ended with one of them having a busted lip or a nosebleed!

Today, Ionescu is known for being a strong player with her left hand. She told a story of Eddy once teasing her about how he was better with his left hand than she was. Ionescu forced herself to play with only her left hand for several days. Her determination to beat her brother helped shape her game today. "And now I use my left hand more than my right," she said.

FACT

Eddy transferred to the University of Oregon before his sister's junior year and shared an apartment with her.

>>> Ionescu shows her ability to play with her left hand in a 2019 game.

CHAPTER TWO

A GIRL WITHOUT A TEAM

By the time she reached middle school, Ionescu had fallen in love with the game. She was excited to play on her middle school team. Then she got the bad news: There was no basketball team for girls. Ionescu asked about playing on the boys' team. "My middle school said I should be playing with dolls," she said in a 2019 interview.

Sabrina didn't give up. She asked other girls if they wanted to form a team to play basketball. She also forced her way into playing with the boys. She would attend Eddy's games and bring her sneakers with her. She hoped they would be short a player and she could get in the game. Sometimes, it worked.

 Ionescu's focus on basketball continued into her high school years.

FACT

Ionescu is ambidextrous. That means she can do things equally as well with her left hand or her right hand.

FOLLOWING HER DREAMS

Even after being told to go play with dolls, Ionescu never quit. When she was 12 years old, she wrote a speech. It was about her love of basketball. She said she was going to keep working to one day become a WNBA player.

It would have been easy for Ionescu to give up. Instead, she worked harder to make her dreams come true. Today, the former number-one WNBA Draft pick is a professional basketball player. But she never forgot what it was like to be told to play with dolls instead of following her dream. "I wish I could go back and just tell those people they had made a mistake," she said.

>>> Ionescu's determination to play her best is apparent in every game.

CHAPTER THREE

HIGH SCHOOL STAR

Ionescu made her high school varsity team in her first year, but she wasn't a starter. Her high school coach said Ionescu sat the bench for the first half of her freshman year. "Sabrina had her share of failures . . . " said her coach, Kelly Sopak.

Eddy told a story of a **playoff game** in Sabrina's freshman year where the failure and determination came together. With 2.6 seconds left in the game, Ionescu stood at the free throw line. She had a chance to tie or even win the game for her team. She missed the free throw. She was heartbroken. She cried. And then, according to Eddy, she went straight to the gym and shot free throws for hours. "Yeah, she doesn't miss free throws very often anymore," he said.

〉〉〉 Ionescu congratulates a player on the other team after a 2015 loss by her high school team.

〉〉〉 Teammates carry Ionescu after winning the open division semifinal game in 2016.

GROWTH IN HER GAME

Once she became a starter, Ionescu quickly became a superstar. Tall players might be great rebounders. Quick players can rack up a lot of assists. Players with a perfect shot score many points. Ionescu could do all three. She said the balance in her game came from playing mostly against boys growing up. They didn't want to pass her the ball, so she learned to rebound.

In sixth grade, she played against much taller players on the eighth grade team. That made shooting difficult, so she learned to be a great passer. Hundreds of hours on the court with her brother made her a great shooter. Ionescu was a complete player. In her three seasons as a starter, Miramonte High School never won less than 30 games. **Scouts** began to take notice. Ionescu's play would soon make her one of the highest rated basketball **recruits** in the nation.

SENIOR SUPERSTAR

Ionescu was unstoppable her senior season. She led her team to the girls' state open division championship game. She also set the record for most points scored in school history with 2,606.

One of the highlights of a basketball player's high school career is getting invited to play in the McDonald's All American Game. Ionescu was named to the 2016 game in Chicago, Illinois. She was matched up against the best players in the country. Ionescu was the star. The game went to overtime, and the teen took over. She hit back-to-back three-point shots to lead her team to a 97–88 victory. Ionescu scored 25 points, a record for the girls' event. She was named the game's Most Valuable Player (MVP).

FACT

In her four years at Miramonte, Ionescu's team finished with a record of 119 wins and only nine losses.

>>> Ionescu holds up her MVP trophy at the McDonald's All American Game.

CHAPTER FOUR

COLLEGE BALLER

Many high school athletes choose their college early. Ionescu was different. She couldn't decide where she wanted to go. She was recruited by many great colleges. Of all the players in the 2016 McDonald's All American Game, Ionescu was the only one who had not yet chosen her college. Finally, in June, she decided she was going to be an Oregon Duck.

Ionescu didn't even tell Oregon basketball coach Kelly Graves she was coming. She just arrived at the school and went straight to the gym to let him know. The next day she began her college career.

>>> After joining the Ducks, Ionescu had many celebratory moments with Kelly Graves (left) and her teammates.

SUPERSTAR DUCK

At Oregon, Ionescu became a triple threat. If teams guarded against her, she delivered a perfect pass. If they gave her space, she sunk a basket from anywhere on the floor. If they backed off once a shot was up, she swooped in and grabbed the rebound.

In 2015–16, the season before she arrived, the Ducks lost 11 games. In her three years as a starter, the team's record was 97–13.

One of her biggest moments came on December 20, 2018. Oregon was crushing Air Force 70–32 in the fourth quarter. Ionescu jumped high to grab a defensive rebound off the glass. The game was already decided, but that rebound put Ionescu in the record books. It gave her a **triple-double**, the 13th of her career. No player, man or woman, had ever earned as many in a college career!

〉〉〉 Ionescu played for team USA in a 2017 game.

Team USA

From 2013 to 2019, Ionescu played in 23 games for the USA national team. The teams went 21–2. As a member of the Under-16 squad in 2013, her team won the gold medal at the International Basketball Federation (FIBA) Americas U-16 Championship. Ionescu won her second gold medal in 2014 when she was a guard on the U-17 World Cup Team. In 2019, Ionescu was a member of the USA 3x3 team that also captured the gold medal.

READY FOR THE PROS

After her junior year at Oregon, Ionescu was eligible for the WNBA Draft. Many experts expected her to be chosen number one. Ionescu shocked basketball fans everywhere when she announced she was going to stay at Oregon and finish her college career. Ionescu wanted a shot to win a national championship. She was willing to risk injury and miss out on the WNBA for a chance to help the Ducks win it all.

In her senior year, Ionescu led the Ducks to a record of 31–2. The team had an opportunity to bring a national title to Oregon. Then the **COVID-19 pandemic** hit. The NCAA canceled the tournament.

Ionescu set records and won every major award her senior season. It was time for her to make her dream come true. She was ready for the WNBA!

>>> Kobe Bryant, Gianna Bryant, and Ionescu appeared in an ad near the Staples Center in Los Angeles, California, during a memorial service for Kobe and Gianna in 2021.

Friendship with Kobe Bryant

On January 11, 2019, the Ducks were playing a game against the University of Southern California Trojans. Former Los Angeles Lakers superstar Kobe Bryant attended the game. Bryant spoke to the team and made a connection with Ionescu. He became her **mentor**. He would text or call her after big games. She worked out with Bryant and his daughter Gianna, who dreamed of playing in the WNBA. In January 2020, Bryant and his daughter died in a helicopter crash. Ionescu dedicated the rest of her senior season to Kobe and Gianna.

CHAPTER FIVE

WNBA ROOKIE

On April 17, 2020, the New York Liberty selected the 22-year-old point guard with the number-one pick in the WNBA Draft. It was a difficult time to begin her career. COVID-19 changed everything. The WNBA pushed back the start of the season.

On July 25, Ionescu stepped onto the court for her first pro game. The long break may have had a bad effect on her skills. She shot 0–8 in her three-point attempts. She was 4–17 overall. The Liberty lost to the Seattle Storm, 87–71.

〉〉〉 Ionescu goes for a shot in her WNBA debut.

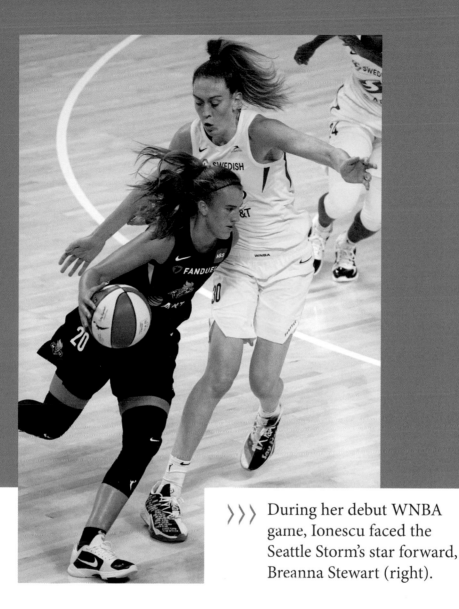

〉〉〉 During her debut WNBA game, Ionescu faced the Seattle Storm's star forward, Breanna Stewart (right).

Ionescu bounced back with a huge game four days later. She scored 33 points and added seven rebounds and seven assists. Then in her third pro game, Ionescu injured her ankle. The **rookie's** season was over after just two and a half games.

FUTURE STAR?

As the 2021 season began, the Liberty were off to a great start. In their first game on May 14, Ionescu sunk a three-point buzzer-beater to win the game over the Indiana Fever. She led her team to an early 4–1 record and was named Eastern Conference Player of the Week. On May 18, she became the youngest player in WNBA history to get a triple-double.

Many fans believe Ionescu will become one of the greatest to ever play in the WNBA. She is still young. It is too early to tell what kind of professional career Ionescu will have. But her fans in New York hope she stays healthy and brings a WNBA Championship to the Liberty!

〉〉〉 Ionescu reacts with excitement after making a game-winning basket in May 2021.

TIMELINE

1997   Sabrina Ionescu is born in Walnut Creek, California, on December 6.

2016   Ionescu is named the USA Today Girls Basketball Player of the Year.

2016   Ionescu wins the Gatorade State Player of the Year for California.

2017   Ionescu is named PAC-12 Freshman of the Year.

2019   Ionescu wins a gold medal as a member of the USA Basketball 3x3 team.

2020   Ionescu becomes the only player in NCAA history to score 2,000 points and have 1,000 assists and 1,000 rebounds in a college career.

2020   The New York Liberty select Ionescu with the number-one pick in the WNBA Draft on April 17.

2020   Ionescu makes her WNBA debut on July 25, scoring 12 points and collecting six rebounds.

GLOSSARY

COVID-19 (KO-vid NINE-teen)—a mild to severe respiratory illness that is caused by a coronavirus

MENTOR (MEN-tur)—a trusted adviser or teacher

PANDEMIC (pan-DEM-ik)—a disease that spreads over a wide area and affects many people

PLAYOFF GAME (PLAY-awf GAYM)—a game in a series played after the regular season to decide a championship

RECRUIT (ri-KROOT)—a person who is asked to join a team; colleges recruit players for their teams

ROOKIE (RUK-ee)—a first-year player

SCOUT (SKOWT)—someone who looks for players who might be good fits for a team

TRIPLE-DOUBLE (TRI-pul-DU-bul)—when a player gets a total of 10 or more points, assists, and rebounds in one game

READ MORE

Chandler, Matt. *On the Court: Biographies of Today's Best Basketball Players.* Emeryville, CA: Rockridge Press, 2020.

Frederick, Shane. *Candace Parker: Basketball Star.* North Mankato, MN: Capstone, 2020.

Jankowski, Matt. *The Greatest Basketball Players of All Time.* New York: Gareth Stevens Publishing, 2020.

INTERNET SITES

ESPN: The Legend of Sabrina Ionescu
espn.com/espn/feature/story/_/id/28878754/the-legend-sabrina-ionescu

WNBA: Sabrina Ionescu
wnba.com/player/sabrina-ionescu

WNBA's 25 Most Defining Milestones
espn.com/espn/feature/story/_/id/31270404/the-25-firsts-defined-wnba-25-years

INDEX

AUTHOR BIO

Matt Chandler is the author of more than
60 books for children and thousands of articles
published in newspapers and magazines. He
writes mostly nonfiction books with a focus on
sports, ghosts and haunted places, and graphic
novels. Matt lives in New York.